Carla's Special Paintbrush

by Joanne Mattern

Illustrations by Marc Mones

Carla loved to paint. One night she dreamed she had a special paintbrush. Everything she painted came to life!

When Carla woke up, she saw something new on her desk. It was a paintbrush. Carla grabbed the brush and started to paint an apple tree.

Once she painted the last apple, Carla
looked out the window and saw an apple tree!
"This paintbrush really is special!" she cried.

Carla couldn't wait to show her paintbrush to her class. Then she remembered it was Field Day at school today. "This is going to be a great day!" Carla said. She got dressed as fast as she could.

At school, Carla showed her brush to the class. "This is a special paintbrush," she said.

"Why is it special?" asked Mrs. Bates, the teacher.

"Whatever you paint comes to life," said Carla.

"Oh, really?" said Mrs. Bates. Carla could tell from her voice that Mrs. Bates thought she was joking.

Mrs. Bates picked up the paintbrush and painted a huge rain cloud. Then she started painting lots of raindrops.

"Mrs. Bates, stop!" Carla said. But it was too late. Just then, the room got dark.

The class looked out the window and saw rain coming came down in buckets. "Oh my," said Mrs. Bates. "The rain will ruin Field Day. We can't play games in the rain."

Suddenly Carla had an idea. "Mrs. Bates, paint a sunny day," she said. Mrs. Bates quickly painted a big yellow sun. The rain stopped. The sky cleared.

"We saved Field Day," said Mrs. Bates. The class cheered.

Mrs. Bates handed the paintbrush to Carla. "Keep this in a safe place," she said.

"I sure will! I might just need it for another rainy Field Day!" she smiled.